Edwin Brand

Mad Authors

Or, Daft Dan's Diary

Edwin Brand

Mad Authors
Or, Daft Dan's Diary

ISBN/EAN: 9783337119461

Printed in Europe, USA, Canada, Australia, Japan

Cover: Foto ©ninafisch / pixelio.de

More available books at **www.hansebooks.com**

MAD AUTHORS:

OR,

DAFT DAN'S DIARY.

MARVELLOUS REVELATIONS RESPECTING
MADHOUSE MANAGEMENT.

BY

EDWIN BRAND.

FOURTH EDITION.

London:
PRINTED FOR THE AUTHOR
BY
ALEXANDER & SHEPHEARD, 21, Furnival Street, E.C.
1893.

(Entered at Stationers' Hall.)

PRESS NOTICES ON SECOND EDITION.

The Editor of the *Kentish District Times* under date Nov. 27th, 1891, writes :—

"Mad Authors; or Daft Dan's Diary" is the title of a curiously interesting story by EDWIN BRAND. It is founded on facts, and in it the author endeavours to bring before the public the many evils from which the victims of insanity suffer. These "marvellous revelations respecting madhouse management," should be read by all who are interested in this important subject, which unfortunately affects one way or another a large portion of the community.

The Editor of the *Cambridge Daily News* under date Dec. 3rd, 1891, writes :—

"Mad Authors; or Daft Dan's Diary" is the striking title of what in many respects is a very remarkable brochure written by EDWIN BRAND. The work consists of a treatise on insanity, the incidents in which, although written in a humorous style, are based upon hard facts. The first edition of the work was sold out in three months, and those who are interested in the many evils from which the victims of insanity suffer—and who is not?—would do well to secure a copy of the book.

PREFACE.

IN introducing this work to the notice of the public, the author begs to state that although the incidents connected with the story are humorously written, and savour much of fiction, they are, nevertheless, "founded on facts"—facts which cannot be denied.

Still, insanity is not a subject to be lightly handled, yet the writer considered that his somewhat quaint style of expression would best serve him in his earnest endeavours to bring before the public the many evils from which the "victims of insanity" suffer.

If "insanity" required "insane treatment," the author's mission would be useless. But when we know that just a modicum of "common sense" would set all things right where patients are concerned, one cannot but wonder at the ignorance displayed respecting their "management."

Your faithfully,

THE AUTHOR.

Contents

Eccentric Authors.
Fairyland.
Daft Dan's Diary.
Daft Dan.
Childhood.
School-days.
Life at the Bench.
Professional Grease-pushing.
Quill-driving.
Ill-health.
Mental Wreckage.
A Grim Spectre.
A Clodhopping Cousin.
The Battle of the Iron Bars.
On the Road to the Asylum.
The Half-Way House.
Beer, Bacca, and Biscuits.
The Home of Insanity.
An Asylum Bathroom.
Clean Clothes.
Patients and Pictures.
Dinner-time (Snail Sauce).
The Story of a Field-day.
Tea-time.

Liquid-loving Lunatics.
Walking the Boards.
An Asylum Somersault.
The Hero of the Hour.
All Jaw and no Jaw.
The Land of Nod.
Bed-time (Comical Lodgers).
Dream Talkers and Sleep Walkers.
Vacant Stomachs and Vacant Minds.
Breakfast (a mild concoction of Cocoa).
Before the Doctor (Charity Chops).
Food and Famine.
The Details of a Diet-Table.
Getting Shadowy.
Work (Agricultural Abilities).
Leather Cases (Leather Unlimited).
Asylum Ales.
Taking a Peep at the Pigsty
Armed Homicides.

CONTENTS—*continued.*

The Wood Shed (Chopping and Chatting).
Lunch-time (the Roll Call).
Brain Food (a Fishy Failure).
Farm Work (Trenching).
A Small Musical Festival.
The Sleep of the Just.
Men and their Manias.
A Strange Starvation.
Birdie "Bright Eyes."
Love's Stratagems.
Defeat and Departure.
Prisons, Palaces, and Public Asylums.
Washing-day (a Bathroom Promenade).
The Weekly Ball (Merry Maniacs).
A Comic Variety Company.
Lodging-house Dustholes.
Country Walks (Fettered Freedom).
Dreary Wards.

Weary Watchmen.
Strange Bedfellows.
A Pauper Lifeboat.
Poor Humanity.
Asylum Hospitals.
A Cunning Bone Worker.
Asylum Sabbaths.
Killing Time with Closed Eyes.
Up to Date.
A Rude Awakening.
A Medical Missive (Love and Physic).
Visiting Day (Promised Liberty).
Crazy Valets.
Before the Committee.
Questions and Answers.
A Small Cash Payment.
Bowing and Bending.
Red-tapism.
Daft Dan's Discharge.
Homeward Bound.

MAD AUTHORS.

Oh, spare a moment from your pleasures, friends,
To mourn with those who wander all alone,
Or, with the phantom forms that madness lends,
Whene'er a noble mind is here o'erthrown.
                                    MARIE ASTON.

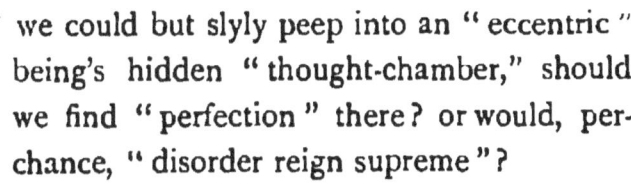F we could but slyly peep into an "eccentric" being's hidden "thought-chamber," should we find "perfection" there? or would, perchance, "disorder reign supreme"?

Surely it cannot be that the world's "eccentric" ones are so mentally organised that they can allow their "minds" to feed upon both "sanity" and "insanity" at will! Most people think so. Well, unfortunately, if it be so, it will curiously enough follow as a fact that all persons of "eccentric" habits are more or less "mad." I cannot pin my faith to so strange a theory. Of course I am not eccentric!!!

And besides, can we possibly view such a queer supposition in the light of an actual truism, when we so well know that "eccentric authors" have ever proved to be our best fiction-writers? And yet some of the "knowing ones" knowingly account for even this fact—they tell us that our "eccentric," or as they would put it, "mad" authors first gained (ages ago) their immense popularity by means of a "fairy bridge." The tale is worth telling. One day (hundreds of years ago, before railways, steam trams, roller skates, telegraph wires, telephones, phonographs, photography, fire brigades, traction engines, and penny-in-the-slot machines, fairly frightened the fairies out of the country) a small band of eccentric authors sought the aid of the "Fairy Queen of Literature."

These sorry scribblers were in a very sad plight. For many years they had been vainly endeavouring to gain fame in the "fickle field of fiction"; hope deferred made their poor hearts sick. The cause of their condition is easily explained. The "pig-headed critics" who reviewed their books always considered that their frequent flashes of "eccentric wit" were entirely due to mental derangement, and, as a consequence, their literary efforts remained unsold; in fact, their reputation fairly rotted under the damning influence of "adverse criticisms."

Few things can be more discouraging or dispiriting to an author than to come across a whole list of hostile criticisms.

Few people are so barbarous as to deliberately pass

adverse criticism upon a *baby*, however ugly and misshapen that infant may be. They respect the mother's feelings, or, at the worst, pass by in judicious silence. But no such mercy is accorded to the literary bantling.

The knives and daggers of inimical criticism are plunged into the heart of the miserable victim, until the unfortunate author fairly writhes beneath the torture, and looks as askance at a stall of newspapers as a dentist's patient at the collection of instruments which have at various times inflicted upon him the most gruesome pain, however humane and considerate the manipulator, or ease-giving the object in view.

Adverse criticisms may be compared to the hornet's sting. Soothing applications in the shape of friendly applause may follow in the wake of the damnatory clauses, like soothing appliances upon the smarting wound, but the pain does not subside at once. Time, the great healer in most cases, has to mow down minutes, hours, and days, to say nothing of the larger crop of weeks, months, and years, before the sensitive soul is at rest again. And hence the plight of the sorry scribblers.

Well, these poor pen-pushers wended their way to "Wonderland." Upon entering the palace of the "Fairy Queen of Literature" they humbly bowed before her throne. They suddenly became so greatly amazed at her marvellous beauty that they almost forgot their errand.

But the Fairy Queen was not at all displeased. Being a woman, she was naturally not averse to a little flattery judiciously administered occasionally. It is to be imagined, indeed, that many *men* do not altogether dislike a small dose of the pleasing mixture, well wrapped up and slightly disguised, though they perhaps wave it aside, as it were, with a deprecatory movement, instead of "fishing for more," like some of their female prototypes. I say *some* advisedly, not *all*. So the good fairy having greeted the pen-pushers with a splendid specimen from her large assortment of bewitching smiles, the poor authors, again bowing low, quietly related their several grievances.

The Fairy Queen lent a willing ear to their doleful tales, and promised to assist them. The poor penmen, again bowing low, tendered her their warmest thanks and hastily departed, considerably cheered and enlivened by Her Majesty's gracious promises. Nor was it a case of "out of sight, out of mind," with her; they were not doomed to wait day after day in dull and dreary disappointment.

In less than a week our book-making brethren received a summons from Spiritland, and thankfully they obeyed the call.

After much toiling, though the way did not seem either so long or so wearisome, now they were so delightfully certain of a charming reception, they again reached the "region of mystery" in perfect safety.

The Queen still occupied her fairy throne; but while the authors were undergoing their usual bending and bowing, the enchanted palace descended to earth. They quickly perceived that they had changed worlds, as they plunged once again into the earth fogs and mist, after enjoying the clear rarefied air of the upper regions, and they began to feel slightly saddened again at the thought of returning to all the grim and sordid details which they had altogether forgotten for a time in the purer regions of Cloudland. Little did they dream of the scene that awaited them. They could scarcely believe their own eyes, and began to think that they must certainly have been invested with magic. spectacles in those fairy realms. As they looked out upon the stormy sea of "public opinion" they found it was spanned by a most beautiful bridge.

Deep down on either side of the "fairy structure" were sharp-peaked rocks—*i.e.*, pig-headed critics. Ever and anon big-jawed fish rose above the water; these were reviews. And so the once sorrowful scribes, being now filled with joy, well knew that they need sorrow no more, for their two greatest enemies—*i.e.*, pig-headed critics and adverse reviews—were now perfectly powerless.

But although the happy authors knew their worst enemies to be safely immured in durance vile, there was still another stumbling-block. As they passed on into the open country, they became aware of a small army advancing to meet them, each man almost bowed to the earth beneath his heavy load. What could it be that overburdened them in this manner? Alas, too soon, far too soon, the eccentric authors were enlightened upon this point, and a thrill of horror passed through their prophetic souls. Each man bore a bulging sack, containing masses of carefully written papers, and all were labelled "Rejected Manuscripts."

Then the happy authors knew that these were *un*happy authors, returning from unsuccessful interviews with that awe-inspiring being—an Editor. And they shook in their shoes for sympathy.

And being in a reckless mood, for there is safety in numbers, they resolved to interview that Editor. So they knocked at the great man's door.

And when he heard that it was a deputation of authors, his soul was wrathful within him. He armed himself with his largest bottle of ink, and strode into their presence.

And when they saw him, they quailed before the power of his eye, and turned to flee, falling over each other in reckless confusion. Then he raised his mighty ink bottle, and hurled the contents upon them in black indelible streams.

They had been "ink splashers" before. They now became the "ink splashed." Howls and groans and prayers for mercy arose from one and all.

With a triumphant shout the victorious Editor returned to his den, and never again was he interviewed by authors, successful or unsuccessful, mad or sane. Wherefore he was profoundly thankful.

But when the authors returned to the sea of "public opinion," with one accord they were seized with a desire to bathe therein. They immersed themselves, and lo and behold! the editorial ink splashes disappeared, leaving not a trace behind.

Their self-respect was restored to them. They emerged from the sea, feeling several inches taller, and proudly rejoined the ranks of successful scribblers. The big-jawed fish had not dared to intrude upon their ablutions; and the sharp-peaked rocks were powerless to hurt them, so securely were they fastened in their places.

All their former deadly enemies were now perfectly innocuous, their claws cut and pared with a vengeance.

As the "happy authors" crossed the bridge, they were welcomed by twelve little fairies, who for ever rang out the world's applause on fashion's fairy hand-bells.

DAFT DAN'S DIARY.

It is well to state that the incidents in connection with this story occurred in the life of a friend—an eccentric one too. We will suppose he is spinning his own yarn.

Knowing that ladies generally condense the most important part of a letter within the narrow limits of a "postscript," I beg to add mine—

P.S.—Wishing to please the anticipated multitudes who will probably read these pages, and feeling sure that a "cantankerous" few will—even in these days of free education—still unblushingly brand the "very eccentric" as "insane," I have, by way of pleasing even these erring ones, obligingly christened the hero of our story "Daft" Dan.

"Daft Dan" is not a very attractive appellation for a true knight of the quill; yet, if my name is not worthy of much notice, nature has more than made up the deficiency, for my features are the "happy hunting-ground" of all rude people. And there are not a few upon this earth of ours, their rudeness taking varied forms.

Sometimes it is unintentional. Then it is pardonable. Very often it is intentional. Then it is unpardonable, or, at all events, blamable.

The magnetic influence which ever causes poor humanity to look and linger is connected with my organs of vision. I do not squint round corners, nor yet wear spectacles, but simply "sight society" with a weird dreamy stare, which may be taken to denote anything or nothing. At the same time, I beg to state that this dreamy stare of mine is a totally different affair to "the poet's eye in a fine frenzy rolling."

If I *am* "daft," I am not by any means given to frenzied movements of any description. Wild whimsical whirlwindish (if I may coin a word for the occasion) whirligigs are not part of my stock-in-trade.

When young, the sports and pastimes which other children enjoyed so much charmed me not. Gaiety could never tempt me beyond the limit of my own little world. I often got laughed at; but being in possession of a small store of nature's own ammunition (biting sarcasm) I frequently silenced my worst enemies; those who came to grin, grinned no more; not in my presence, anyhow. Physically, I was not strong; mentally, I was not weak: in fact, my brain was far too active, and I far too often accomplished that fool-hardy feat known as "burning the candle at both ends."

I was often away from school, through ill-health, but when able to study, I learnt quickly.

After leaving school, I had a fleeting fancy for cabinet-making, so, seeking out a cunning worker in wood, I "began life at the bench." It is not all "beer and skittles" running a half-rip saw through a beech board, neither is it "all pie" handling a Jack-plane.

Possibly I lacked energy and could not muster the necessary "go," anyway, of one thing I felt quite certain, I was never meant to make shavings. Of course I didn't "Jack" up the job without giving it a fair trial, but finding that the chips and sawdust which I manufactured during the day (and I never manufactured anything else) visited me at night in the form of a nightmare, I thought it was best to clear out, and, if possible, take my next mania to a better market.

For my next venture in this work-a-day world I chose art, the art of "French-polishing." This quiet occupation was more suited to my contemplative mind. I found that "hand and brain" could work in unison. Very often while my hands glided mechanically over the surface of the wood, my busy brain worked out problems.

But I did not labour long as a professional grease-pusher; the constant smell arising from the polish began to affect my health, so, taking the timely advice of a man of medicine, I hastily departed for the sea-shore. Change of air worked wonders, so after a little beach-walking, boating, and bathing, I made tracks for home.

Being dead sick of art, and "dead nuts" on trade, I embraced literature. Fiction writers do not always ride in Fashion's phaeton. Struggling quill-drivers seldom think about "fame," but simply write to avoid "famine," which is a slightly different thing. The merry chink of the "almighty dollar" sounds just as musical in the ears of a poor author as it does in the aural appendages belonging to the "more cunning cranium" of a wealthy stockbroker.

I had but just netted a few pounds through the power of my pen, when I again became suddenly ill: "the Fates were against me." My life had never been "a bed of roses," but it was now veritably "a bed of thorns."

* * * * * *

Once again I dodged the cruel hand of Death, and once again the Fates were against me. I feel sure even now that my bodily vigour would have been more quickly restored if I had not been overtaken by a new dread, the dread of "going mad."

It happened this way: One day the doctor was paying me his usual morning visit, when I accidentally overheard him whisper three terrible words, "County Lunatic Asylum." I at once connected those words with myself, and wove them into a fearful phantom, which haunted me continuously, night and day.

No one, perhaps, who has not experienced that awful dread can know how terrible is the overhanging fear of insanity.

At first the victim is only partly conscious of the few slips he may chance to make, but as the fell disease makes rapid headway, the doomed creature all too soon realises the awful fact that, so far as this world is concerned, himself and happiness have dissolved partnership, and parted company for ever.

No human being can possibly undergo a more trying ordeal. True, a few stedfast friends may perchance dole out to the unfortunate one a full measure of sympathy, but, alas, pity only tends to make the maddened brain more maddened still. To a maniac, the word "friend" has no meaning. Being unfortunately, through his terrible disease, a fiend himself, he verily believes that all humanity is fiendish.

But still, if there cannot be a bright side to insanity, there certainly exists one less dark; for a merciful Providence doth sometimes (perhaps, to our way of thinking, far too seldom) step in. and kindly soothe the tortured fevered brain by producing a long lapse into unconsciousness, and so under this new influence the one-time raving one sleeps as calmly as doth a little teething cherub under the composing influence of Mrs. Winslow's soothing syrup, and frequently in the maniac's case, the benefit derived is even more lasting, simply because his haunted mind ever more lacks activity.

Aye, even "grim Death" itself need not walk in slippered feet, for the maniac remains all unconscious of his sure coming.

Yet again, other victims of this fell disease appear to live in a little world of everlasting mirthfulness, their lives being like one long ripple of laughter on a sea of happiness.

This is the kindliest way Providence has of easing human beings of their many responsibilities; at least, so think many overburdened tax-payers.

Ah! misfortune and its twin sister poverty stalk forth in many disguises, and although their visits may be short ones, they are, none the less, not easily forgotten. Truly, riches make unto themselves wings and fly away; health may be our portion to-day, illness to-morrow. A body racked with pain is a burden almost unbearable, but to possess a mind which makes life one continual nightmare, is to know that such a one has reached the utmost limit of human suffering.

As previously mentioned, those three terrible words, "County Lunatic Asylum," haunted me continually. I looked upon them as Dante's characters in the "Inferno" must have gazed upon that awe-inspiring inscription, "All hope abandon, ye who enter here."

This terrible sentence seemed written in letters of fire across my weary brain; but yet I could not, I dare not, allow myself to think that I should ever degenerate into a poor sorry occupant of a County Madhouse. I knew that my nerves were much shaken, and that I was also a bit run down as regards health, but yet for all that there appeared to me a very wide gulf fixed between nervous debility and downright madness. But alas, *my* train of thought and that of my guardian relatives were certainly not running on parallel lines, in fact the danger signal was up, and there seemed some risk of a collision. As events proved, I could not keep my liberty, or my faith in human nature, always excepting a certain little homely maiden, of whom more hereafter.

This ever-present horror—the "horror of insanity"—clung so closely to me that it seemed to form an inseparable part of my very being. I tried to administer a false peace to my weary mind, but my poor heart refused to be comforted. At length, however, a little ray of bright sunshine pierced the clouds that were now overshadowing me.

One day I received an unexpected visit from a distant relative (as I was given to understand), a country farmer. This kind individual actually invited me to share the unlimited space of his large farm-house for an unlimited season. The prospect of the near approach of a long holiday buoyed me up wonderfully; only one thing marred my joy.

This clod-hopping cousin of mine appeared to have suddenly dropped from the clouds, for when I questioned him respecting other members of our family he was perfectly dumb. I made one sorry attempt to draw him out (as I thought) from his usual atmosphere of "pork," "cabbage," and "potatoes," but it was no go; it was merely casting pearls before swine. He might pose as an interesting "son of the soil," but he would never be a "society man."

There is "a skeleton in every cupboard," and there was still one in mine.

I had foolishly imagined that my somewhat renewed health had entirely "laid" the terrible ghost that had hugged me so closely (the ghost of despair), but I was mistaken, for the grim spectre was still grasping me. Yes, truly enough, I had yet to fight, and yet to fall, in the dreaded battle of the "Iron Bars" (the County Asylum).

Although my anticipated "change of air" still buoyed me up, I frequently suffered from severe mental depression.

"Coming events cast their shadows before." The date

of my expected journey came round at last. I shall never forget the morning of that day. During the preceding night sleep entirely deserted me; therefore I rose unrefreshed. My mind appeared to be filled with a strange presentiment of coming evil.

Over and over again I called myself a "fool," and tried to act wisely, but it was no use. Just then one of my relatives entered the room. She kept so pleasantly chatting about the holiday in store for me that I actually felt almost happy.

At last I was again left to myself, and to my own reflections. But it happened most fortunately that I had no time to get melancholy, for my ever-listening ears suddenly caught the ominous sound of approaching wheels.

Still, I was not so much put about, for the neighbourhood in which I resided was not one of the "grandest," it was not considered very aristocratic, so I merely imagined that the rumbling noise proceeded from the parish dust-cart busy with its usual calls. However, I thought I might as well satisfy my curiosity; it would certainly help to kill time. Did any of my readers ever strain their eyes through a muslin curtain? I performed that somewhat remarkable feat that morning. And what do you think the straining process revealed to me? A carriage and pair at my own door.

Now, I scarcely expected that my "dung cart benefactor" would arrive in such state, neither did I expect that victims of insanity were ever driven about in four-wheelers. Well, I got rather mixed, and finally felt very suspicious.

Not wishing to be seen from the window, I wended my way to the door-mat. I crept along the length of the passage as silently as a slimy snail; then gently kneeling down I surveyed the "arrival" through the rusty surface of the front door key-hole.

My little peep-show was not a success, for all that I could discern was three brass buttons, and a small watch chain.

Presently, a sharp rap from the heavy knocker quickly brought me to my usual position; I arose from the mat in great haste. Flinging the street-door wide open, I calmly scrutinised the face of my "friend"—or "foe."

We did not beat about the bush. I asked him his business, and he told me his mission. It was a fresh-air mission.

Yes, he was the "agricultural affair" whom my (supposed) relative had appointed to land me safely at his "lone farm house." So I was now off for my holidays.

As we entered the vehicle together, many people much

wondered why "Daft Dan" had been so suddenly honoured with "carriage company." But I was not one bit abashed. I lounged back upon the yielding surface of the well-stuffed cushions as naturally as though I had been "born to the purple."

"Judge not a man by the coat that he wears." My travelling companion proved to be one of nature's true gentlemen.

Yes, beneath the rather coarse clothing of this man, existed manners most marvellous. He must certainly have kissed the "blarney stone"—he was so charmingly chatty.

Away we sped along the "Queen's highway," quickly leaving "London Town" behind us. As we reached the country roads, our horses slackened speed, but our tongues slackened not.

Presently our conversation turned from gay to grave. We were busily discussing the well-worn subject "Metropolitan Pauperism" when our horses suddenly halted at "The Half-way House."

My friend being rather deaf we mostly talked with bowed heads, so the unexpected jerk arising from the stoppage of the carriage caused us to play a pleasant little game at "touch noses."

At this noted hostelry—"The Half-way House"—my

bill of fare consisted of three courses—"beer, bacca, and biscuits"—all free of charge, waiter included. Very soon we were again on the road; my friend was as charming as ever. By way of change, our conversation chanced to turn upon money matters. Well knowing that my purse was not over-filled with the "necessary needful," I remained almost silent. My friend, noticing my apparent apathy, kindly asked if my mixed diet had caused indigestion. I merely replied that I felt a bit sleepy, but still wishing to continue sociable—and not knowing anything to talk about "cheaper" than the weather—I remarked upon the beauty of the day. In a few minutes we again pulled up; our pleasant journey had come to an end, and so had my happiness.

A man in livery opened wide a creaking pair of strong iron gates. Looking from the windows of our conveyance, I found we were passing along a smooth broad road, which led—not, as I supposed, to a nice farmhouse,—but a veritable prison. Still, I did not take in the situation of events all at once, for the huge building reminded me more of a well-windowed workhouse than a County Asylum, but when I caught sight of the iron bars, which "grimly guarded the glistening glass," I knew, as if by instinct, that I was about to be cut off from the rest of the world, and that I should, in all probability, end my days in the dark home of insanity, a "sorry maniac."

Just then I heard the noise of the clanging gates behind (another patient admitted).

The ominous sound of the closing gates seemed to ring out a cruel death-knell to all my hopes.

* * * * * *

I passed the doctor in the usual way; he, of course, went by the certificate (relating to my insanity) which had been duly signed by a medical man—therefore I had no voice in the matter.

A man—or, pardon me, a "gentleman"—connected with the Asylum (called a charge attendant) requested me to accompany him. As Paddy puts it, "I footed mesilf after him like a born bog-trotter," and travelled by his side until we both reached the bath-room. At the word of command, I undressed, and instantly sought oblivion in the watery depths of the washing machine (the warm bath).

After going through the usual process of washing and drying, I felt defiant. Only fancy! Daft Dan defiant!

The attendant then conducted me to a large cupboard; I had already received a "clean shirt," I was now awaiting "clean clothes." I was very soon the unhappy possessor of a very "unsuitable suit." The garments strongly reminded me of the old song, "Days gone by";

still they possessed one redeeming feature—they were well acquainted with the wash-tub.

Now the man who previously inhabited those clothes was a giant, that's certain! For ye see, they did not rest equally upon the surface of my carcase anywhere, but merely touched me here and there, making me feel for all the world like an animated rag-bag. As for my hat, that crowned the lot, it fitted me like a bird-cage.

Well, I paced up and down the length of the ward like some "deck-treading" sea-captain anxiously awaiting a storm. But at last my promenading began to grow monotonous, so I quietly sat down.

Getting rather tired of doing nothing, I went in for surveying first the patients and then the pictures. The patients certainly looked more interesting than the pictures—at least, I thought so.

However, my stock-taking was very soon abruptly ended through hearing dinner announced. One thing, you could not very well mistake the name of the meal you were about to enjoy, for the attendant kept bawling it out like a "loud-voiced bloater-seller."

We all took our seats at a long table. The feed in store for us consisted of three courses, not "beer, bacca, and biscuits," but "pork, cabbage, and potatoes"—ah, stop a minute, though! I was quite forgetting the intermediate course—the cabbage was served up with an attachment of snails. Feeling sure that snail-sauce was a sure cure for insanity, I devoured the slimy relish with a contended spirit. Having greased our appetites and watered our drink-a-tites, we again said grace.

After dining so heavily on such real country fare—" pork, cabbage, and potatoes "—I required a "constitutional" to walk it down. As luck would have it, it was our "field-day," so you may assuredly guess that I was well pleased. I had previously imagined that a "field-day" was a kind of holiday—a sort of "gala day"—a day on which folks generally muster for some special sight-seeing. I knew that society often visited Volunteers' field-days, and they might visit ours. I did not know—I hoped they would, anyhow.

Now, don't you think, dear readers, that I was sadly discomfited when I was given to understand that our "field-day," being interpreted, simply meant "a day in a field," with no other earthly attraction than the sorry sight of a few attendants playing cricket? That was our field-day!

But, worse still, I was not allowed to enjoy even this little spectacle. Would you believe it? An insane asylum bye-law (much more insane than *one* of the patients, at all events) actually debarred "fresh patients" from enjoying "fresh air," simply because they were "fresh patients." Hardly creditable, is it? And yet most assuredly true.

Well, it was not "Daft Dan's" day out after all; and well he knew it. However, not to be sold completely, I queried like this—the next best thing to "going to a fair" is to "hear about it"; so with this intent firmly fixed in my weak mind, I sought information. I quickly chummed up to a dear creature who was—for the time being, like myself—a close prisoner. I could not have hit upon a better party, for he was knowledge itself where "field-days" were concerned.

Naturally enough, I much wondered how he, to me a fresh patient, should be so much "in the know"; but, alas and alack! the tale is soon told—he was a new arrival for the third time; thrice had he been incarcerated within the self-same walls.

My fellow-prisoner was very loquacious—he was a born orator. His tongue must most undoubtedly have been hung clean in the middle, for it kept continually clapping at both ends.

Never before was I ever under the complete spell of so talkative a maniac.

As regards myself, I had no need to ask questions; so soon as he became acquainted with the nature of the information required, he went right through with it—he "knew the ropes" so well.

I think it is better that I should detail my "field gleanings' in my own language.

During fine weather those patients who possessed sufficient nerve-power to well withstand the intense excitement which always accompanied an "Asylum cricket match," were allowed to look on — very few played.

To me, the game appears to be got up for the entire benefit of doctors and attendants. The wickets are generally pitched before we (the patients) enter the ground. As a rule, the doctors start the batting, and the attendants the bowling. As a class; the attendants are very pliable under the will of their masters; hence the doctors' many runs, and the attendants' bad bowling. Sometimes, for a few minutes, a couple of the weak-minded will stand in front of the wickets, and busily belabour the ball, but such a sight is very rare, and does not often occur. A lunatic's conscience requires a lot of training before it will allow him to deliver a ball to suit the skill of a superior, I can tell you!

Now and again, too, some sorry patient will follow the ball when it comes in his way, and when he sends it home, the players generally thank him with almost as much energy as a lazy man gets up with. To my friend's thinking, the only time when the fun comes in, is when a patient, instead of making a run for the ball, runs for his liberty—and he frequently gets it, too!

Yes, many an asylum inmate has, for a short time,

enjoyed freedom through escaping from a cricket field. But, as a rule, the poor fugitives are soon recaptured; their scared faces and "Noah's Ark" regimentals (asylum clothes) soon cause them to become a prey to some passing policeman; and then, when they are brought back, they have to submit to a course of discipline more severe than ever.

Yet some patients, when escaping, get miles away, even reaching their own homes. But when they chance to arrive at the family hearth, they seldom figure as welcome guests, their room being generally much more desired than their company. The more especially so when the escaped one visits his nervous loved ones in the dead of night. For once in a while, the smaller members of the maniac's family do not look upon the touching lines of the old song—"Father, dear father come home"—as a chorus worth realising; they even wish father farther.

Escaped lunatics, naturally enough, are not long harboured. They are, as a class, much dreaded; but still not always deservedly so. I may venture to assert that many a male ward in a county mad-house frequently possesses its full complement of inmates without possessing a madman—they are all perfectly harmless. Just as my friend finished his tale—a rather long one—he was suddenly called upon to exchange wards, and I have never seen him since; an asylum friendship soon vanishes.

Clatter! clatter! clatter! Such was the noise the wanderers made, as they ascended the staircase when returning from their "field day."

Wishing to appear friendly, I addressed one of them. I am still awaiting his reply; he has never yet spoken.

Feeling a bit hurt at such strange treatment, I began to get mopish; but I did not mope long.

Coming across another patient, I approached him more carefully. I took a dive into my talking stock-pot, and fished up the weather. I had not been mistaken in my man this time, nor yet in my subject. "Weather" was his strong point. He was well up in the state of the weather almost from the time of the flood.

"Tea, oh! Tea, oh! Tea, oh!" So cried a loud-voiced attendant, and so to tea we went. Each patient received a small block of bread, very scantily buttered.

A long row of pint mugs (brimful of hot tea) also awaited us. My late slimy diet having caused me to feel a bit thirsty, the sight of a big drink proved doubly welcome. After washing the snail tracks away from my throat, I felt much better

To my great surprise, we received another visit from the man with the tea-can Being still dry, I again soaked my inner man with a second dose of suction. I had always imagined that tea-drinking was nerve-shattering; but be that as it may, the nerve-affected family were certainly used to the liquid, for I saw many a crazy customer do his full quart comfortably.

I may here remark that most (if not all) of the attendants have "seen service." Why soldiers should offer themselves so freely for such monotonous work I cannot understand.

Once again I walked the boards; up and down the ward I toddled. My walking-tour was, however, quickly ended through my turning a complete somersault over a large zinc pail, brimful of hot water. I received a thorough good wetting.

As I stood there, with clouds of steam ascending from my garments, I might have been easily mistaken for "a piping hot soup kitchen."

The man with the mop kindly asked me to "move on," so I slunk off; but I dare not sit down for fear of making an impression, so I stood it out.

Getting wet through in a dry ward did not end comfortably. The patients who had not witnessed my late disaster, could not account for my watery condition; so they began plying me with all sorts of questions. I was the hero of the hour.

At length, feeling myself a fit subject for a "sit down," I dropped into a seat, and finally dropped off to sleep.

Sleep had scarcely spread her welcome mantle over my tired brain more than five minutes, when I was again brought back to things earthly, through a fellow-patient kindly offering a small pipe of tobacco. Not wishing to offend "the least of one of these my brethren," I went in for a whiff.

My good-natured chum proved to be a man after my own heart. He was something of a cross-breed between "all jaw" and "no jaw." I enjoyed his society very much.

Again feeling rather drowsy, I entered "the land of Nod," and actually experienced happiness in a madhouse. Yes, I had a dream, a happy dream! I dreamt that I was free; but when I woke, it proved a joke, for "bed-ho!" greeted me. Yes, I was rudely awakened through hearing the ever-recurring sound of "bed-ho!" as it echoed through the ward; and so to bed I went, but not to sleep.

I was placed in a small dormitory in the receiving ward; we were six lodgers "all told." During the night, nightmares were prevalent; somnambulism, also, was well represented. I arose in the morning unrefreshed, but still undaunted. "Daft Dan" still remained desperate.

To while away the unearthly hours preceding breakfast, I sought comfort in scrubbing. As the fifth lot of dirty water was gently leaving my bucket, I very much wondered which of the two complaints was really the most endurable, a vacant stomach, or a vacant mind, and came to the conclusion at last that the former might be the more easily filled.

Relief came at last, breakfast was ready. Grace being ended, we quenched our thirst with a mild concoction of cocoa. No doubt the cocoa itself (apart from the water) was really good, but like all good things in this world, it appeared mighty scarce. It was certainly so weak that it seemed scarcely equal to the exertion of crawling down our throats. The usual block of bread and butter awaited our arrival—one block for each blockhead. Feeling somewhat refreshed, I arose from my seat, and assisted the man who was mug-gathering. As I followed the creature who carried the crockery, I felt as though I might be twin-brother to the biggest "mug" in the building.

During the morning I was again inspected by the doctor. He was a thorough practical man. If an inquest had been held over my body that night his treatment of my case would have been entirely beyond suspicion, for he simply ordered me a "mutton chop lunch"; this little kindness expired at the end of a week; I never received a charity chop after. I suppose they had the kind intention of "letting me down gently." While conversing with one of my numerous friends, I learnt that those patients who were strong enough to work, received extra allowance. "Bread, cheese, and beer" was served out to those who laboured; but as regards the incapable and weakly ones, they generally went *minus* (unless medically privileged).

Sunday was recognised in the asylum as God's day. It was not *our* day, that is certain. Therefore, workers ceased from working, and lunchers ceased from lunching. Every man (I don't know about the women) was then tarred with the same brush—lunch time was only known by its entire absence. This struck me as being decidedly different to the usual rules of society, Sunday diet, in ordinary cases, being superior to the fare customary during the remainder of the week. However, I was beginning to discover that ordinary rules were not to be met with in this grim abode.

For fear my readers may think that I am making mountains of mole-hills (respecting our diet); it is necessary to mention a few facts:—

We receive three meals per day—breakfast, dinner, and tea (no supper). At 6 a.m. we leave our beds. "Bedlam is then let loose." Fast-breaking commences at eight: this repast consists of hot cocoa and bread and butter (one slice only). One o'clock brings dinner, a fairly good meal, except fish days—fish dinners are failures and our repasts were not exactly of the "whitebait at Greenwich" order. Then comes the usual tea-drinking dissipation (5 p.m.) accompanied by the usual "one slice only." Now, are we not aptly styled a "famine-struck" family, considering that we only receive two slices of buttered bread from one dinner-time to another? Quite one-half of the patients are compelled to exist on this scanty fare.

As regards myself, not being able to draw sufficient sustenance from our "insane diet-table," I daily became more shadowy, and having no wish to regain my freedom by way of the grave, I determined to work and go in for the extras. Being duly informed that the charge-attendant "bossed" the labour department, I hied me to him, and humbly placed my flesh, muscles, and bones at his disposal. About the two former there might be some doubt, but the latter spoke for themselves, and spoke very plainly too. They were so very visible. The charge-attendant seemed scarcely able to realise the fact that my attenuated form was still capable of making work scarce ; but my urgent appeal went straight to his heart, and he closed with my offer at once.

When, on the following morning, the "farm hands" were collected, I found myself among them. It is quite true that my agricultural experience was not of a high order, for it had simply begun and ended in one sorry attempt to grow "mustard and cress" in a flower-pot; but what mattered it? I knew I had gone in for ruralizing, and therefore must abide by it. Our ganger, after running his eye over his motley crew, led the way.

Upon reaching the lower depths of the stone staircase, we "booted" ourselves.

Never such shoes as those shoes, surely, thought I; for they were composed of "leather unlimited." In some manufacturing towns, there is an old adage "nothing like leather." There was certainly nothing like those. Each patient made haste to handle the pair that best fitted him. I, with my usual amount of good luck, came in for the last pair, and they happened to be "odd ones," probably by way of upholding the Asylum reputation for "oddities."

"Well, being now well encased within my "leather cases," I awaited the signal to depart. Off we went, "flippity flop," "flippity flop"; never before was I a member of such a brigade, and never since; it is fortunately a limited privilege—a privilege which few enjoy.

As we travelled along, I endeavoured to study the geography of the country. After traversing the paths of some well laid-out gardens we came upon more open scenery. The first building we passed worthy of notice was a big brewhouse. Of course, "asylum ales" are only intended for home consumption, they are not yet in the open market ; and if they were they would quickly become a drug, because "asylum ales" do not contain sufficient alcohol to tempt ordinary mortals to imbibe them.

Closely adjoining the brewery were the gasworks— "light" is essential even to lunatics. Afterwards we reached our coal depôt—even crazy people can well appreciate the comforting warmth of a good fire. Victims of insanity would most assuredly create a fuel famine if they were allowed the run of the coal-box, they are so much addicted to big fires, ever bright and blazing. The carpentering, shoemaking, and tailoring shops were closely clustered around the main building. I also noticed a fireman busily engaged in the examination of some new hose.

When we think of some two thousand partially helpless creatures completely enclosed within a small world of their own, all right-thinking persons must certainly decide that a fire-engine is a necessity. The attendants frequently attend fire drill. Fire-quenching being a tricky business, practice is essential.

Upon veering a little to the right we came upon the farm proper. Taking a peep at a pig-sty, I noticed that the pigs were well cared for. But, alas! like all other pigs, a cruel fate awaited them ; they must eventually "die" that we might "live." But then, simple-minded swine are, fortunately, born fatalists— they have never a care for the future.

I don't know how it was, but after leaving the pigs, I turned a bit poorly. I felt strangely sick and strangely strange.

I seemed all at once to more fully realise the stern fact that I was an entire stranger in a strange land—a stranger among strangers, in fact.

My thoughts now began to wander back to home, but they never really reached there; for just then my foot wandered upon the pointed surface of a long rusty nail inside my boot (forgive the term "boot"! it happens to be the handiest, and it boots not which I use, if I make myself understood). My late disaster quickly diverted my rapt attention from home thoughts to present misery; I suffered severely.

Having at last reached a small rough-looking "shanty," we came to a halt. After unlocking the door, an attendant presented each patient with a peculiar-looking implement; we each received a keen-edged chopper.

I must confess that I handled my "murderous weapon" with a firm grip, yet for all that, I fairly shook in my shoes, foolishly imagining that we had all been seized with "homicidal mania," attendants included.

However, my mind quickly became a bit more settled when I took in the true nature of events; we were not expected to pose as "mighty warriors," but simple "woodchoppers." Yes, we were destined to spend the next few hours in the asylum woodshed. The time I spent among my "brother chips" was lively in the extreme; we "chopped and chatted" to our hearts' content. Still, apart from politics, I would rather do a twelve-months' tree-felling with the "Grand Old Man," than accept a guinea an hour as an "asylum woodchopper."

And so my tongue wagged, my hands worked, and my eyes revolved in their sockets, ever watchful lest some accidental blow from a fellow axe-wielder should cleave my cranium, for maniacs are not given to "straight blows."

We were well supplied with sharp-sighted sentinels. Ever and anon, the now well-known tread of the watchful attendants attracted my attention as they kept constantly pacing to and fro in front of the building. Yet I cannot understand why one was not appointed to do duty inside. But no doubt discharged soldiers much prefer "small talk" to shavings.

"All things come to those who wait," and so it was with me; for just as my nature required sustaining, the Asylum clock struck "eleven," which, to us toilers, meant "lunch-time."

At the welcome sound of "beer, oh!" we immediately left our business and filed up to the little shed which previously held our choppers. Here, as we answered to the roll-call, we rushed to receive our "lunch dole." The eating and drinking was fairly distributed. After imbibing a couple of tots (half-pints) of fresh ale, besides disposing of something more solid, I felt refreshed, and returned to work with a lighter heart. No remarkable adventure or misadventure occurred to me during the rest of the morning. I believe, after lunch, we were less chatty, if anything than before, which does not speak well for "Asylum ales" anyhow.

One o'clock relieved us from our toil. After safely consigning our keen-edged cutting tools to the tender care of one of the keepers, we fell in, and marching on again reached the "home of insanity," where dinner awaited us.

The first course, the last course, and the only course served up for dinner that day was "fish." Of course there are fish and "fish," coarse fish and fine fish, fleshy fish and flabby fish; our fish was very "fishy"; such a peculiar consignment from the watery depths was really worth beholding.

Now most folks consider that (well-conditioned) fish food is "brain-strengthening." Agreed; but unfortunately for us Asylum inmates, our universal providers continually tried to educate us up to the peculiar idea that evil-conditioned fish was the most nourishing. Yes our so-called benefactors (our caterers) appeared to believe that strong-smelling fish was the most sustaining—we didn't; it might be the cheapest—more smell, less money. As a fact, if we had chanced to be a benighted drove of "Thames water-rats," we should have believed ourselves at Billingsgate; the air of our great London Fish Market was never more fishy.

This powerful form of highly-scented "brain food" was not well received by any of the inmates. Strong language kept continually issuing from between their teeth; I am not in a position to mention which of the two was the strongest—the scent of the "fish" or the "language."

Fortunately my constitution had been previously fortified by my "little extras," so I, unlike many others of the dinnerless family, was the better prepared for so disappointing a diet.

After about an hour's rest we again mustered for outdoor labour. I beg to state that our "leather cases" were duly awaiting us at the bottom of the staircase—of course we could not dine in those shoes. The line must be drawn somewhere as regards "etiquette," even in an asylum; we drew it at boots.

The rain had now ceased descending, and we were again enjoying "fine weather." As we tramped wearily along I fell a-thinking that most likely I should soon enjoy my first spell of farm work. On looking around,

I quickly discovered that our dear little "beer shanty" was fast fading from sight; this was not comforting. But knowing that there are more ways of "killing a cat" besides "hanging her," I thought, probably, our suction travelled with us.

Yes, I was quite right; there was still a weak-minded brother among us, equal to bearing the heavy burden of two huge bottles. So far, so good; now for "muscle-moving."

I received my spade with a feeble sigh, not feeling quite equal to the effort of using it. We were all set to work, like so many soldiers, "trenching." In case some of my readers may lack wisdom as regards trenching, I will briefly explain—the earth, by means of a spade, is gradually thrown up, each clod being gently laid among its fellows, until the ground assumes the happy appearance of a well-ploughed field.

Although the work is apt to prove monotonous, it is easily performed.

Our taskmasters were not hard on us; any movement of the body, however far removed from hard work, fully satisfied them—in fact, anything short of standing still was, with us, "time well spent." The attendants themselves generally started a gossipy confab respecting the general management of our menagerie. If "stand at ease" meant "stand and freeze," they would certainly stick to it.

Well, after grubbing up the ground for about a couple of hours, we all cried "a go," and left the clods to take care of themselves for the rest of the evening.

Before retiring for the night, we were graciously favoured with a small musical festival. Naturally, the centre of attraction was the band—two musicians only—bandmaster and baton both absent; what a sorry spectacle!

Yes, two attendants did the music, or over-did it, I am not certain which; while a few patients cut some queer capers on the surface of the floor. Then we had some singing. I am not sure who did that—I didn't; I had never posed as a " public singer " in my most palmy days, let alone then.

However, our entertainment, if not fashionable, was certainly not dissipating, for we sought our pillows at the usual hour—*i.e.*, 8 p.m.

That night I slept beautifully; whether all agriculturists sleep so soundly I cannot say. Probably not, in bad harvest times, when either hay or corn is in danger, from the destructive elements. One thing you see—we were not harassed with such harassing matters as tithes, taxes, and rent-charges; our liabilities were limited.

" Men and their manias." Different people possess different manias, and yet the same person often possesses different manias at different times, that is to say, a person may be constantly chatting one day, and entirely mute the next.

Brain ailments are quite as complex in their nature as diseases of the body; hence arise the varied forms of derangement from which the "weak-minded" suffer.

In my opinion, the most troublesome of the mania-suffering tribe are those persons who are afflicted with "cantankerous manias." They are not only under the spell of the disease themselves, but the suffering they inflict upon others almost equals their own. Whenever "two or three" are gathered together for a friendly chat, he, the cantankerous party, swoops down upon them. No matter whatever the nature of the subject under discussion may chance to be, he always "begs to differ." Of course if his begging to differ were politely performed, one could bear with him. But no such thing. If a person could swallow his adverse opinions as fast as he gave them, he could digest his own coat-tails.

The "cantankerous maniac" constantly uses all manner of subtle means to wriggle himself into your good graces; but woe be to the party whom he thus beguiles, for as soon as you venture an opinion of your own, he fairly "sits on you," and finally crushes you under the overwhelming weight of his own great importance.

On the other hand, if you allow the cantankerous creature to manacle you, and make you his slave, the case is no better; because, ever after, whenever he finds you busy with gossip, he will track you about like a born " thief-catcher."

And another thing; the fellow will never allow you to ignore him, oh no! I have frequently offered him the " cold shoulder," but he never yet took it; in fact, if the mania is well developed there is no cure for it.

I cannot fully describe the many manias which flesh is heir to, the task would be too tedious; but still, before dropping the subject entirely, I will mention one more.

" A strange starvation." Very few persons would care to witness the daily sufferings of a human being who persistently refuses to take food. Yet, unfortunately, such a sight is frequently witnessed by attendants in most public asylums. Very often the person who becomes a prey to this terrible mania has previously enjoyed good health; a case in point:—

A railway porter, stationed at a busy station, was one day seized with a great loathing for food; he also displayed a great lack of energy; failing to get better, he sought medical advice.

On arriving at his home (he was a married man with a small family) he hourly became worse. His poor wife was greatly alarmed at the nature of his illness; he would not allow even the smallest amount of nourishment to enter his lips.

Railway porters as a class do not command large incomes; so, as he daily appeared to become more feeble (both mentally and physically), his loving wife sought the only shelter she could find for him—the "Public Asylum."

It is needless for me to relate the many preliminary arrangements which preceded the afflicted porter's due incarceration in his unlooked-for prison-house.

The iron gates of the "County Asylum" readily opened to receive him. Would he ever pass that way again? Who could tell?

I cannot but mention the praiseworthy efforts made by the attendants to induce the poor fellow to eat.

The only way of prolonging the life of such a man is by "tube-feeding," and this was, in his case, fully resorted to; but a "food-forcing apparatus" never yet effectually barred "grim death's advance," for if the treatment be continued, the "patient" soon dies. The poor suffering porter was frequently visited by his wife and little ones. I will just mention a most touching incident. One day the wife prepared, as a last resource, a most dainty morsel. Packing the appetising fare snugly away in a small basket, she visited the Asylum.

The fond wife did not start on her mission of mercy alone, she was accompanied by the smallest portion of her small family—"little birdie bright eyes."

After waiting awhile in the visiting room, the door gently opened, and in came—not the muscular form of an obliging railway porter, but a "human wreck." As she surveyed his wasted figure, the wife could scarcely recognise him as the one-time bread-winner of her little family.

Little did this self-sacrificing wife and mother guess how soon the weakened life-link which bound her to him would be severed; already, even as she stood there, the loving bonds of holy matrimony were being gently loosed by the clammy hand of death.

It is almost impossible for me to describe the painful scene which followed.

Quick as thought, "little bright eyes," "daddy's best beloved," climbed upon his knees.

Now, "little birdie bright eyes" was a born strategist. After entrenching herself in her father's affections, she used all love's many stratagems to win back his appetite.

Oh, how anxiously the fond mother watched the wily movements of her little daughter as she persistently pressed " dadda " to eat.

Love's warfare still raged, and still the mania remained master.

Surely the angelic form of little "bright eyes" was best fitted to become victor; surely she would not fail.

Truly it was a hard fight. Many that day were the fruitless journeys those little hands made to "save father," and yet she still remained dauntless; verily, she had learned her lesson well.

Doctors had already failed—utterly failed—in their dealings with the disease. Would "bright eyes" fail also? Yes, amid a very deluge of hot tears, she failed too! Such is the power of so terrible a "mania." The quivering voice of our "child hero" was now silent, she was simply vanquished through "sheer exhaustion;" her strength was gone.

It is not well to prolong such harrowing details. Suffice it to say, mother and daughter returned home, and the poor porter went home also; he quickly journeyed from "earth's platform" to a better land.

* * * * * *

A public asylum is, in many respects, far worse than a prison, because "patients" (unlike prisoners) never know when the term of their imprisonment is likely to expire. They may "do a short stretch," or they may "do a life stretch." They cannot tell—such is the uncertainty of asylum law—"language without love."

Well, where's the remedy? Close at hand! If when the doctors saw their patients' minds mending, they held out to them the blessed hope of renewed freedom, it would act like a charm—many poor sufferers would then regain lost liberty a great deal sooner.

Of course, there is an exception to every rule; one cannot lay down a hard-and-fast line for the treatment of insanity, certainly not. Discretion is most necessary when dealing with brain ailments, and who so discreet as a doctor! ! ! Facts are stubborn things. There are, at this present moment, hundreds of poor patients now breathing asylum air, who will for ever breathe it, so far as this world is concerned. Let us hope that to them Death may indeed prove the Gate of Life. But they will continue in hopeless incarceration here below, unless doctors be more agreed that the plain meaning of the little text, "hope deferred maketh the heart sick," is still worth following. All medical men (outside asylums) give "convalescent patients" encouragement. Very often the doctor's smile is more healing than his medicine. Brain diseases not only require medical attendance, but medical attention also; success does not lie in the many visits, but in the power of the visiting.

* * * * * *

The next item in the week's programme was washing-day, so the weak-minded brethren were now called upon to exchange the comforting air of the well-warmed ward for the chilly delights of a weekly wash. After scampering helter-skelter down three flights of well-worn steps we reached the bathroom. Each patient was then expected to undress quickly. I fell out of my clothes in less than a minute. There were about twenty baths ready for use, and about forty patients ready to use them. In less than a jiffy a score of the nimblest were wildly embracing the water. Not being very fleet of foot myself, I shiveringly joined the waiting "shakers."

We began to shake all over the shop, then we started a "bathroom promenade." Presently I left off footing time to the musical splash of the water and fell out of the ranks.

I had just espied an "empty bath," in fact, the end bath had not been occupied. So delighted was I with the prospect of being covered with warm water, that I almost "shook hands with the steam."

In I jumped, the liquid was exactly the right heat, the temperature thereof made my poor heart glad.

Before going down in the watery depths for the third time, the "boss of the washhouse" kindly requested me to turn out. Having learnt my church catechism to some good purpose, I endeavoured to obey. While busily rinsing out the soap from the corners of my eyes, I felt as if I were being slaughtered with a keen-edged knife. Wishing to seize my would-be assassin as quickly as possible I immediately turned round. I soon perceived that I was not suffering from the dreadful effects of a sharp knife, but from the equally cruel effect of a sharp east wind; it was blowing upon me through a broken window. Surely, thinks I, as regarding the patients shunning this bath, there certainly exists "a method in their madness."

A smart rub down with a rather wet towel soon caused my blood to circulate more freely. In a few minutes I was fully dressed and ready to depart.

On the way back to our ward we passed through some small "airing courts." The dreary courts were then unoccupied—insanity had deserted them.

At night I attended the weekly ball. Here "mirth and madness" reigned supreme.

The "Asylum Band" was in attendance. Gaily danced the merry maniacs, each one endeavouring to keep step with the uncertain sounds which proceeded from the instruments. Not being able to do the "light fantastic toe" myself, I formed one of the "non-dancing community," and took my seat in an "upper gallery."

Looking down upon the "madding crowd" below, I became greatly interested in their weird movements.

Of course, the attendants who formed the "band" were not considered "insane"; yet, as I intently watched their peculiar manners, and listened to their peculiar music, I certainly thought that their mental condition required "classifying."

After retiring from the ball-room, we retired to bed. Oh! stop a minute, though! I had clean forgotten the "cake and coffee"; this little feast was served out to us on "dance nights only."

Next morning each patient became a member of a "Comic Variety Company."

The order went forth that we were each to be clothed with an "additional shirt." We entered into our extra arrangements without undressing. The attendants were similarly attired.

There we stood, almost motionless! Just like a long row of "double-shirted sign-boards." At last the ward door was thrown open,—and we were fairly trapped. The passage ceiling and walls required "scraping"—(they were about to be freshly coloured) and we were the expected "scrapers." What a sell!

Each patient being armed with a sharp tool, we commenced operations. It was a dusty job, and no mistake!

I unfortunately was told off to work with the gang below, so of course we received all the refuse from the gang above.

Our mouths were quickly filled with dust and dirt; in fact, I got in such a filthy condition, that a fellow-worker actually mistook me for a "lodging-house dust-hole."

The day following, we were favoured with a country walk. (My readers will probably recollect that "Daft Dan" was a thorough believer in "fresh air missions.")

As we left the asylum the attendants gave up their keys to an officer at the lodge gates. We did not march in any particular order, but wandered all over the pavement. We might have been following the track of an "escaped serpent," we did so shockingly shamble.

Well, I can only speak of this country walk—this "shackled slaves" holiday—as a very disappointing affair, for although we enjoyed the fresh air, we did not enjoy real liberty; our freedom was still fettered.

Ever after that memorable outing, the daily grind at the asylum seemed doubly irksome. I felt as if I had now reached the lowest level in the social scale—the dead level of a living lunatic.

Our wards and our watchmen. When patients first enter a county asylum they are immediately examined by the doctor. This personal examination, coupled with the (not always truthful) wording of the parish doctor's certificate, frequently enables the medical gentleman to classify them at once.

Sometimes, however, some patients, through possessing "doubtful" or "ever-changing" manias, cannot be thus so readily classified. All such folk are quickly drafted into the " receiving ward."

After remaining in this uncanny structure (under so-called close observation) for a short or long period, they finally occupy some other ward where the discipline enacted is more or less severe, as their cases may require.

To my way of thinking, no better preliminary abiding place could possibly be found for such a " mixed host of sorely-stricken mind-wanderers."

But alas! owing to want of discretion on the part of those possessing authority, the wrong patients are frequently placed there.

For instance, it often happens that newly-arrived patients are, for the time being, merely suffering from some very slight ailment, the effects of which would, if the patients were wisely placed among happy surroundings, quickly pass off. But the slightly ailing ones are, unfortunately, not so placed, but are, on the contrary, miserably imprisoned within the "receiving ward," where dwell, as previously stated, " poor creatures, who unknowingly possess ever-changing manias."

Now, as these "dear changelings" frequently lapse into a fearful state of real " frothy madness," it will be plainly seen that within this ward the "comparatively sane" and the " completely insane " all live together.

This should not be so; such an unhappy state of things ought not to be long countenanced. There cannot possibly exist a more baneful or dangerous practice. One can easily perceive that placed as I was, within the narrow limits of a small receiving ward dormitory (with a brain as active as the supple limbs of a modern lamplighter), I endured martyrdom. Almost nightly, always weekly, fresh lodgers with "undecided manias" inhabited our bed-chamber. Rest, which to me in my case was so essential, was never mine. Frequently we had (by loud knocking) to seek the aid of the patrolling watchmen, so that they might turn out one or more of our newly-arrived "ferocious lodgers" into "single cells," there to vent their unwonted wrath upon bare walls and vacancy. Besides, the hideous night scenes which nightly takes place in asylum "receiving wards," to a convalescent patient the "day scenes" also are most terrifying, for one never knows how soon some seemingly mild-tempered lunatic may change into a "murderer"—this is not comforting.

I do not think that the lives of lunatics, who live under so-called "close observation," should be so frequently used as "tempting baits" for would-be homicides. It is not my wish that anyone should for one moment unjustly suppose that a "murder" could actually be perpetrated within a "receiving ward" without the attendants observing it; certainly not. The little incident would, as a matter of course, be observed and also duly reported, and no doubt the assassin would then be the more easily classified ; and there, so far as the patients are concerned, the "murdering" would end, until another tragedy chanced to follow close upon its heels.

Curious to relate, our county asylums vary almost as much in the manner of their formation as the lunatics themselves.

Some asylums, when built, form so many blocks, while others, when erected, contain as many angles as an oldtime gridiron.

Yet some of our more modern madhouses look quite cheery when viewed from a distance ; and yet again, others of a more ancient date are so devoid of all architectural skill that they would most decidedly form apt models for lone paupers' tombstones.

It is hardly necessary for me to state that all asylums in a finished condition are "roofed in," but there the comparison ends. For the interior of each building is so differently divided and sub-divided, that to adequately describe each one of them would take up a lifetime.

I also feel quite sure that my indulgent readers do not wish Daft Dan to wander all over the basement of the asylum again, merely for the sake of the better explaining the exact measurement of a few petty offices ; neither is it well that I should waste my time " sniffing " the air of the cookhouse.

If a patient chances to be the happy possessor of a "good dinner," it suffices him, he has no wish to pry into the trade secrets of the kitchen; and if he did so pry, no doubt the knowledge gained would only tend to make his little meal all the less enjoyable. It is one of those cases in which "distance " most probably "lends enchantment to the view."

The receiving ward has already been described; but not sufficiently so. This ward contains—firstly: attendants quarters' (single rooms), also one or more small dormitories; then follow single cells, small bathroom, padded room, lavatory, and scullery. Here, as in other wards, the weak-minded ones manage to eat, drink, and ought to sleep their sorry time away.

In this asylum all the other wards are similarly divided, but they all differ from the receiving ward in one respect. In these wards the meals are not so much hurried over, or so roughly served—a great advantage surely, where bad teeth or a weak digestion are concerned—and I do know, for unfortunately I possess both.

Asylum wards are, for the sake of convenience, always numbered, and I, also for the sake of convenience, will name the "better class" ones, convalescent wards. These wards, as their name implies, are intended for the use only of those patients who are happily hastening towards recovery, and so they are as a consequence less noisy, and in fact in every way better suited as a place of refuge for convalescent patients.

The weakest go to the wall here, as in other places. Yes, those weak-minded creatures who finally lapse into a state of "raving madness" have their quarters also. These poor souls are always grouped together in those wards where the discipline enforced is of a necessity most severe—too severe, sometimes.

I think I will now more fully describe our sleeping apartments.

Generally, the largest dormitory in the asylum is, sad to relate, set apart for "epileptics only." In this, the "epileptic ward," the gas is always kept steadily burning the night through.

Here the persons in attendance have a busy time of it.

So many poor sufferers, constantly suffering from the effects of fits, more or less severe, require much attention —careful attention too.

And as persons, when seized with this dread malady, keep continually groaning, this ward also is but a poor place to rest in.

We will now quietly enter the Hospital Ward. If we

visit this ward at night, we find that few beds remain vacant.

Nor can we expect that such beds ever will remain vacant, so long as the people's fight for daily bread daily grows fiercer.

Death, truly enough, by so frequently claiming its many victims, empties many beds. But when we know how the always stormy sea of life becomes so constantly lashed into mad fury through the ever-recurring whirlpools of "over-population" and "keen competition," we must candidly admit that death's task of sick-bed emptying must ever prove a hopeless one.

Yes, "poor humanity," when once engulfed in life's sea by its many whirlpools, quickly becomes, mentally and physically, a living mass of hopeless wreckage, drifting about hither and thither, ever seeking a safe anchorage.

And if by chance the "wrecked ones" are at last rescued by a "pauper lifeboat," they quickly find that they have only been saved that they may be once again more cruelly submerged within the deeper depths of some "Pauper Asylum."

Next, in due order, comes the "Observation Ward." The lodgers who nightly inhabit this huge dormitory do most certainly require much watching.

When some of them sleep I know not, for they seem to

be continually twisting, turning, and jabbering the whole night long; in fact, their nocturnal habits are so dreadfully bewildering, that I find I cannot possibly describe them.

No doubt it will come upon some of my readers as a surprise, that those patients who are under the influence of "suicidal manias," mostly occupy the snuggest ward in the whole building—and the quietest too. Doubly blessed are those folk.

I suppose, as the "would-be suicides" find it utterly impossible to commit suicide every night, they wisely defer the occasion, and as a consequence, sleep calmly.

During the winter months the "suicidal family" nightly enjoy the pleasant warmth of a good fire.

The attendants who are "told off" to attend to these patients are not in the least afraid of them. As these strange customers generally deliver their usual threatenings in the same language, they get used to them; in fact, so much so, that all the "good-nights" ever uttered could not possibly soothe the attendants' oft-times tried nerves more effectually.

Still, none the less, they are well watched; the attendant keeps his eye on them.

Each time, after hustling up his flagging fire, he always stows his poker away in some safely-locked hiding-place; a wise precaution, no doubt. But I think, for all that, there is still room enough left for displaying a little more caution.

For instance, during my incarceration in this, the "suicide ward," I nightly reposed, sometimes snugly enough, just below a long row of gaily-painted flower-pots—they stood on the window-sill, and I lay beneath them.

Well, some nights I would lie awake, much wondering which of the two missiles, a poker or a flower-pot, would prove, if used in actual warfare, the most dangerous, and I generally came to the same conclusion—that, for long range practice, I should prefer the "flower-pot," but for close quarters, the "poker."

Now, I daresay some people would almost prefer spending the night in some dark damp dungeon, rather than in a padded room. Well, let me tell you that padded rooms are not such dreadful places after all. Many a weary patient sleeps more peacefully in such a "room" than does a monarch in his palace.

Most poor sufferers, after their unfortunate fit of raving has subsided, calm down quickly, and as a padded cell is almost "sound proof," they sleep well, and so, after enjoying such a prolonged course of much-needed rest, they soon come round again. Of course some patients simply use a padded room as a last halting-place, ere they journey to the grave; they do not always recover. But, as the saying goes, "If you give a dog a bad name you might just as well hang him," and so it is with padded rooms, they already possess a bad name, and it will ever stick to them. The floors of some asylums are constantly kept well waxed. This more advanced system of asylum floor cleaning is certainly preferable to the everlasting scrubbing process.

Because, if it happened to rain "cats and dogs" on the usual "scrubbing day," which it frequently did (for scrubbing day was every day, or nearly so), the poor inmates were, if not engaged with brush and pail, continually hustled from one end to the other, and, funny to relate, the dear creatures were for the time being (on scrubbing days) just like so many ducks, they persistently paddled "to and fro" wherever it was most watery.

Doctors, and more especially "attendants," frequently become insane through daily witnessing so much madness. But, as a rule, a prolonged holiday, if taken in time, mostly puts them right again, but not always.

Those patients who may be both able and willing to make labour less plentiful easily find employment.

There are always plenty of odd jobs knocking about the institution if an inmate really wishes to seek their acquaintance.

By way of explanation, I will mention a few. As I, "Daft Dan," am well domesticated, I will, like a good housemaid, "start the broom." There is sweeping, scrubbing, perhaps waxing, dusting, window-cleaning, bed making, boot cleaning and stove polishing etc. And as regards skilled labour (apart from farm work)—I do not think that clod-hopping is considered "skilled labour" after all though, is it? Of course it isn't. I'm getting a bit mixed, but I'll go on anyhow.

Well, there is brewing, butchering, baking, shoemaking, tailoring, carpentering, upholstering, painting and whitewashing, in fact, there is work for all, skilled or unskilled. And I must say there is plenty to amuse, if patients be so minded. I will just run over the "dissipations" that are most patronised—billiards, bagatelle, cards, draughts, and dominoes.

Books and periodicals as well abound in abundance, but the most sought-after item of literary fare is the "daily newspaper."

We likewise derive some comfort from our plants, pictures, and cage-birds; but it is necessary for me to add that all these things would most decidedly be the more enjoyable if we only enjoyed our senses.

When, after a severe engagement on some foreign battle-field, we read the list of our killed and wounded, we are apt to imagine that we know the worst—but it is not so.

If an anxious enquirer wishes to more fully know the

vast amount of suffering which ever accompanies "all fiendish wars," let him most carefully overhaul the wards of a few county mad-houses.

Most surely will he find hidden away among the inmates a strangely scattered host of brain-wrecked soldiery.

Aye, victims wrecked to suit a wily ruler's will, or else to satisfy a nation's greed, yet seldom wrecked while justly guarding hearth and home. Yes, truly enough, the fag end of many a brave regiment may be found bravely awaiting death's advance in English pauper asylums.

Is it not also sad indeed to see a one-time valiant, but now weak-minded, soldier, laboriously signing his name as a formal receipt for a well-earned pension, his only witnesses the asylum doctor and a few gaping lunatics.

And to know as well that the small dole awarded him for, perhaps, many years of "hard service," will to him bring no manner of comfort.

As a matter of course, if his pension were big enough, he would not be so cruelly pauperised, but, as it is, if he be married, the wife probably claims the pittance, or, if he be not married, the county grasps it; anyway, the old warrior ends his days as a pauper patient, and finally occupies a pauper's grave.

Night watchmen. Night watchmen who earn their daily bread by nightly perambulating the dimly-lighted wards of our county asylums, are a class of people not to be envied.

These sorry caretakers always travel two together Their mission is to everlastingly tramp from attic to basement, and from basement to attic the whole night through. When the gas is turned down low in the deserted wards and weird windy passages, it is then indeed, without a doubt, the "witching hour of night." Add to this the often unearthly echoes of mingled cursing, yelling, and groaning, which so incessantly issues from the fertile lungs of so many lunatics, not forgetting that the watchmen are supposed to open the door of each cell, and flash the light of their lantern in the not always pleasant face of each maniac, and you have the thing complete without the trouble of witnessing it.

Sometimes, too, a crafty creature, upon hearing the well-known tread of the approaching watchman, leaves his bed, and then slyly hiding behind his door makes ready for a bolt, so that immediately the key turns, off he goes.

These little "night adventures" frequently cause much trouble, both to themselves and the watchman. But any punishment they receive, does not often deter them from attempting the same feat again—even the same night, if possible.

* * * * * *

The amount of ingenuity and patience which some patients display, is really most marvellous. Frequently a far-gone lunatic watching his opportunity, adroitly steals a "likely bone" from off the dinner-table, and then after secreting his stolen treasure for a short time he brings it forth, and by the aid of a worn and rusty nail carves the bone into a most beautiful piece of workmanship.

If you silently watch this cunning workman, as he works away under such almost unheard-of difficulties, you will, if he chances to meet with some untoward accident, see him at his best.

Yes, if he, by some unlucky stroke of his rudely-fashioned tool, mars his work, he does not fret or repine, oh no; but on the contrary, upon ascertaining that the mischief done is quite beyond repair, he wisely bows to the inevitable, and trotting off with a fund of patience not half exhausted, seeks another bone, and having obtained it, smilingly starts his weary task afresh—a capital object lesson for all our lazy ones.

Spending a Sabbath day in an asylum is not all sunshine. We rise in the morning at the usual hour (6 a.m.).

After a slight wash and a great amount of waiting we sit down to breakfast. The meal over, we quietly don our "Sunday suits."

Being now religiously dressed, we await morning service. Some patients wait patiently, others kill time with closed eyes. I, being still of a restless disposition, commenced to count the window-panes. However, my lesson in arithmetic never got finished, for just as I was adding up the first window for the third time chapel was announced.

Now, of course, most ordinary nineteenth-century mortals well know that custom hath it that when a private individual, or corporation, erects a "sanctuary" for religious worship on State Church principles, the said building, through not possessing full church privileges, is designated a "chapel."

But yet, for all that, I am quite willing to unblushingly avow that even I, a cultivated "up-to-date" lunatic, did so far sufficiently err when the sound of "chapel oh !" greeted my ears, as to actually believe that I was, for the time being, about to be a happy "chapel-goer." Imagine my surprise then, when on taking my seat in the holy edifice, I again listened to a "State Church service."

"Cheer up, old fellow!" So spoke the charge attendant, as he handed me a letter, and I did "cheer up" too, for my letter informed me that I should shortly be visited by a dear loving friend.

We terrestrial mortals scarcely ever enjoy complete happiness for any length of time. The loving friend who penned my letter was a lady. She was one of those "feminine arrangements" who "rarely travel." Now, if she had been a "girl of the period"—one of those creatures who can whistle "Yankee Doodle," and "fry a pan of sausages" all in one breath—she would have spared me much trouble. But, as it was, she expected me to furnish her with a detailed account of the various "trams and trains" she would have to occupy before reaching me; a lively job for a lunatic, certainly!

"Faint heart never won fair lady."

Let a workman be ever so good, he cannot work without tools; neither could I write without a "scribbling kit"—pens, ink, and paper. Oh, how I wished I was sitting at my own desk!

A patient, in answer to my enquiry respecting the writing fluid, kindly informed me that the necessary "pen and ink" generally reposed on the "top shelf in the pantry."

"So far, so good, but how about the stationery?"

"Why," said he, 'the charge attendant is always good enough for a sheet of paper and an envelope, providing you ask him pretty."

Well, having gathered together the "needful necessaries," I commenced my letter. For a time I got along "swimmingly." I mentioned the "starting" and the "stopping-places" of the different trams right enough—I knew them by heart—but I stuck fast at trains. I was very deficient in "time-table lore" and no wonder, for I had not heard a "steam whistle" for four long months.

However, I brought my lengthened scrawl to a happy ending, by subscribing myself (you know) in the usual way.

Just as I was giving my envelope a good "licking" to make sure of it "sticking," an attendant coolly remarked: "Your letter must remain unsealed; it has to be read by the doctor."

Now, I may just as well "let the cat out of the bag" at once, and have done with it. I had been writing to please my "sweetheart," never once thinking of the doctor. What a shame! "Love's labour lost!"

The next day I procured fresh stationery ready for a "fresh start." This letter proved a most miserable failure.

Ever feeling that the doctor's eye was on the track of

my pen, I kept constantly mixing fond love with physic. How I managed to so far wade through my "medical missive" as to decently sign myself "Yours devotedly, Daft Dan," I know not.

You may guess how anxiously I awaited my true love's reply. I was half afraid she might mistake my epistle for a "medical certificate"—or it might read like a "marriage certificate" for all I knew. I dare not let her know that "old pills and potions" had anything to do with it. If she had known that her lover's latest love tale had been overhauled by a doctor, she would never have perused it. She would rest herself calmly enough on a "second-hand chair," but she would not read a "second-hand love letter," I assure you.

But putting my trust in the old "saw," which truthfully says "what the eye does not see the heart does not grieve over," I rested contentedly, and in due course the post brought me "glad tidings."

Yes, my domesticated darling (my intended) intended to start on her "mission of mercy" at the appointed hour, trams and trains permitting.

Visiting day (like all other days) came round at last. In the early part of that day I was almost beside myself; in fact, I felt just like a "blind cat on hot bricks," I could not rest anywhere. Most of the patients shunned me like a "spectre," for, weak-minded as they were, they got sick and tired of my continual chatter; "visiting day" was for ever in my mouth.

Presently, the well-known sound of my own name resounded through the ward, it was the signal for my departure.

Upon reaching my "happy hunting ground" (the visiting-room), I quickly espied the face of my visitor. Having lots to say, and knowing that time was precious, we did not stand upon ceremony. Arms and tongues became fully employed, "enquiries and embraces" entangled each other. At length we began to act a bit more rationally—we went in for business.

Love works wonders, and "my love" worked her way into the doctor's dingy sanctum. Yes, she "bearded the lion in his own den," and when she emerged from his majestic presence, she was the happy possessor of good news; she knew that her captive lover would be released in a few days.

This was doing business with a vengeance and no mistake. To say that we were both happy would be talking like a fool; never did a dictionary ever contain a "ghost of a word" which could possibly describe our present delight.

Oh, how I pitied those patients who were less fortunate than myself. The bare idea of their prolonged (or everasting) captivity completely unmanned me.

"Time and tide wait for no man." Slowly, but surely, the merciless hand of the Asylum clock approached the hour—the "dreaded hour"—the "visitor's vanishing hour," and just so surely had we approached the limit of our gossip, so amid heaps of kisses, fond farewells and fountains of tears, we gently separated, I to go from whence I came, while my "loved one" departed a "free agent."

When I returned to the ward, I felt fairly "fagged out;" so much so, that I dropped off to sleep. While thus dozing I fell a-dreaming. After a while my disturbed sleep suddenly became more fully disturbed through hearing a heavy fall. The unexpected noise instantly awakened me. I saw lying at my feet a small parcel. I recognised it immediately; it was a package I had received from my late visitor. When I sat down it was safely lodged within the ample folds of my huge waistcoat, the only luggage department I possessed.

Being now thoroughly aroused, I untied the knotted twine and began to investigate. You could have bought the lot for about half-a-crown anywhere.

"Love's little pair of homely hands" had quietly left me her latest bit of dough-punching, two homely cakes, that was all. Never was "bride cake" handled more tenderly. I soon perceived that my floury treasures had well survived their fall. "Dough-cakes" don't break anyhow, that's certain! There was neither a crack nor a currant in them, nor yet a "plum." They were homely cakes—cakes that could be eaten at any time—cakes that would never cause a "nightmare."

Then came the rub, what was I to do with them? My coat was pocketless! The only safe receptacle that I actually possessed was my own throat—what a pity!

As there was no other apparent hiding place for them, and wishing to end my extreme anxiety, I gathered together a "few guests," a few choice appetites, and so, while thinking of the giver, we "gormandized" the gift. How horrible!

Knowing that freedom was not far distant, I gradually became a new man; my previous woe-begone looks entirely deserted me.

At length the day—the welcome day of my discharge—dawned upon the earth, and my gaze again rested on my own garments.

"Too many cooks spoil the broth!" I was soon surrounded by a small crowd of "half-crazy valets," each one endeavouring to undo what the other had just done; and so, after enduring an almost never-ending amount of much waiting, much toiling and much fingering, I became "fully dressed," a genuine sample of insane handiwork.

Being now in my right mind, with my right clothes on, I considered my captivity ended; but not one bit of it, for I found to my dismay that I had yet to pass the most trying ordeal of all. I had yet to pass the Committee. The doctor, after again testing the contents of my "knowledge box" again considered me a fit subject for freedom, and as such recommended me to the Committee's notice for immediate discharge.

The Committee was composed of a number of gentlemen who were more or less inquisitive. The right worthy chairman was distinguished from the rest through possessing a handle to his name—by way of a title.

On the chairman's right sat the well-known boss of the medicine shop (the medical superintendent). On his (the chairman's) left, comfortably seated, was the burly form of the big local brewer. Why the great brewer should leave the beery atmosphere of his own brewhouse for the purpose of examining my "brains" after a "learned doctor" had twice pronounced them perfect—will, to me, ever remain a mystery.

One would think that the united verdict of the group assembled, small fry included, would either for ever make or for ever mar the doctor's standing reputation as a keen "brain mender." What a farce!

I have yet to mention the actual whereabouts of a most peculiar personage.

On the chairman's left, close to the brewer—whether by accident, or design, I can't say—sat a "suspicious-looking party" with a face like brimstone.

I scarcely know how to classify him—he seemed to be something of a cross-breed—a something between a retired mendicant and a "wealthy match merchant," I could not say which; and so, as I was not able to draw the exact line between refined "beggary" and pure "brimstone," I used much caution, and acted accordingly.

As I stood facing the ponderous form of the burly brewer, I must admit that his peculiarly stolid-looking countenance did not compare favourably with the cheerful aspect of many old ladies when tea-drinking. He was the heaviest swell on record.

However, as he is but a poor tradesman who cannot live without running a fellow-tradesman's goods down, I will take warning, and drop the brewer and the "beer question" altogether—and stick to my book. I am afraid I am getting too personal.

The worthy chairman was the first to challenge me His question was "short, sharp, and simple."

"What is your name?"

Feeling sure that my farewell to exile depended upon the success of the answering, I not only pronounced my name as distinctly as possible, but also as loudly as possible, fearing that some of the Committee might be slightly deaf; for if poor " Daft Dan " suffered defeat through a fellow-creature's deafness, it would be sad indeed!

As my name did not appear to meet with a ready reception, I imagined they failed to compass it, so, not to be found wanting, and being ready armed for almost any emergency, I commenced spelling it—letter by letter.

But my little spelling lesson was never completed, for my feeble utterances were soon drowned by a second question from the chairman; his power of voice was, without a doubt, quite sufficient to swamp the whole alphabet.

Question No. 2 came as a surpriser! " What brought you here?"

You see, I was not certain whether the question really referred to the "circumstances" or to the conveyance, but knowing that to me hesitation in speaking meant bad business, I replied briskly, " Ill-health."

"Ah! you're not looking very well, even now," responded Mr. Chairman.

Directly this truthful remark fell from his lips, I brightened up immediately, for I well knew that if I could not go in for good looks, I must not look " glum"; that would certainly prove fatal. I had no wish to prolong my captivity through my "facial appearance" if I could possibly avoid it; that was another "wrinkle."

Question No. 3 was no doubt intended for a "twister."

"How long have you been here?"

How long! True, "prisoners" often scratch the term of their imprisonment on their cell walls, and each morning when rising scratch one day off; a dreary way of detailing a total, surely!

But I had no need to work out such a sorry time-table.

The "hand of time" might some day, in the far distant future, sponge from my memory (my "mental slate") the record of my captivity; but at present I could easily read it, even without glasses.

I, in reply, stated that I had been incarcerated within the asylum for nearly six months, "country walks" included.

The Committee appeared to treat so short an exile as a mere passing trifle. They considered I had hardly "been there."

Ah! time may fly with some folks, but it does not fly where prisoners are concerned, I can assure you! especially when the prisoner chances to be a crimeless one, like poor "Daft Dan."

I had not even the sorry consolation of knowing that I deserved incarceration.

They, the Committee, seemed to imagine that an ill-fated convict spins out his lengthened stretch of "penal servitude," or an equally unfortunate lunatic his spell of imprisonment, as merrily as they spin out their own favoured lives.

Verily, these committee men seem to possess but few ideas that are really original. They appear to fish out a few old-fashioned maxims from their grandmothers' stockpots every now and again, and it suffices them; they are miles behind the times they live in.

I feel sure that if they were to lose the whole grand total of their best ideas in a fair-sized hay-stack, they would never find one of them, they are so small.

It is one thing to sate oneself with an occasional committee lunch, afterwards favouring insanity with the usual "walk round"—and quite another thing to be shut up within the crazy old castle entirely. "Experience" will sometimes make even "fools" wise, but not always. Question No. 4 came direct from the brewer in good condition.

"Have you been treated kindly during your stay here?"

Well, you see, such a question as that left a wide margin for a patient's mind to travel in: there are so many degrees of kindness, degrees which are as wide apart as the poles, and as opposite in their effect upon the human systems as sugar and vinegar.

Persons (not patients) have even been killed with kindness, when it has been put on thick enough.

Still, killed by kindness may not in the far future be such a rare verdict, where asylum verdicts are concerned; "strange things" do happen, even in the "very best of families;" "pigs may fly" yet, but it's not at all likely.

The brewer's kind enquiry is not yet disposed of. It happened most fortunately for all concerned, that I was in one of my very best moods just then—a forgiving one. So I therefore did not dilate upon my many fits of indigestion, which had been mainly caused through eating strong smelling fish, badly served; neither did I enumerate other small grievances.

In fact, for the time being, I even forgot the great sin of the doctor as regards his wickedly prying into my unfortunate love-letter.

Yes, for the time being, I forgave them all.

I must just add, that, apart from "good moods" or "bad moods," all good-natured souls must know that patients who face the Committee awaiting discharge, frequently manufacture such answers as will best aid their escape from bondage, never once thinking of their consciences; and no wonder, either, when one thinks of the fearful fate they are trying to flee from. And, besides, there is something else to be thought of; we are all acquainted with the old saying which pertinently says —little children and fools always speak the truth; that is certainly worth studying, at least I thought so; I didn't want the Committee to think me a fool, did I?

But leaving fools and falsehood clean out of the question, I have always had a proper regard for truth, even when before a Committee. Yet I must admit that my "answering" that day would scarcely have hung upon the "skirts of truthfulness" if they had not been long and slightly elastic.

Well, I must again tramp back to Question No. 4 —the question of treatment—I had almost forgotten the subject! Pigs don't always stick to one trough, do they?

I duly informed the assembled gentlemen that I had no wish to complain about anybody or anything that was at all connected with my enforced stay in the home of insanity.

That was not saying much in favour of asylum hospitality, was it!

The worthy chairman now graciously asked if I had any work to go to when discharged?

The good man's inquiry was readily replied to, for I

well knew that whenever I sought refuge among pens and paper I could always find employment; employment which generally created a fair income—not affluence, oh, dear, no; affluence will ever be a complaint of the future with poor " Daft Dan."

The big brewer smiled so benignly upon me when he heard of my prospect of sure work, that I imagined he must have mistaken me for an "old customer"—a rather "crooked" one too! one of those customers whose "little bills" habitually represent more goods disposed of than paid for; a numerous class, surely!

Now, if I had been really indebted to the brewer, he would certainly have got the "grin" of me, for even his "beery brains" were equal to the effort of compassing the fact that "work certain," meant "sure money"; therefore he would have hunted me up accordingly. "Back debts," like dead horses, are best got rid of.

After this "little body of modern brain-testers" (the Committee) had duly indulged in a small amount of subdued whispering, the worthy chairman quietly handed me a small "cash payment."

When I gazed upon the proffered coin, I was "fairly fogged."

The worthy chairman had "taken the wind out of my sails" this time, and no mistake, but I did not intend to be caught napping, for all that.

Yes, I was now standing between "two stools," and would most likely fall to the ground.

We all know that it does not do to "look a gift horse in the mouth"; that's right enough as far as it goes, but mine was such a curious dilemma.

I reasoned like this. Is the money being presented to me merely for the cunning purpose of testing my credulity?

If so, when I hold out my hand to receive it, they will dub me a "lunatic," and send me back from whence I came to "wither everlastingly," to lie and rot in "durance vile" for ever.

And again, on the other hand, if I refused such real tangible generosity—"ready chink down on the nail"—my fate would be no better, they would still consider me a "noodle" and a "numskull." I did not know what to do. I could not believe that a madman ever earned real money, or, if he did, I could not believe he ever got it, especially when it had to be sifted through the "large holes" of a keen "committee sieve." I could not believe that!

Oh, my dear readers! what a relief I experienced when the generous gentleman gently hinted that the "trifle offered" would assist me in paying my fare home. I knew he was not befooling me then. Joy of joys!

Oh, yes! I was always open for ready cash—ready money and no humbug—I was always open for that!

The worthy chairman now ended the "interviewing" by bidding me one of his "great good-byes," just as if he meant it, a regular "ear-splitter."

Sometimes a "good-bye" means "a good riddance"; perhaps his did—who knows?

The "small fry" assembled (the lower grade committeemen) took up the strain, and at once forwarded me their "best blessings"; and I, in response, treated the entire company to a limited number of my very best bows, beginning at the doctor (the chairman had been already thanked, especially so) and ending at a little man who was partly occupying a "too big coat"; a "hall-thief" would never have known he was really there, he was so "shadowy."

Still, even now, I had to undergo a little bit more "red-tapism" before I could honestly call myself a "free man."

The charge-attendant, after giving me a gentle nudge, directed my course to a small office closely adjoining the entrance hall. An "authentically arranged" writing factotum (a "sleek clerk") at once asked a few questions, which were not difficult to answer. Having satisfied his clerkly curiosity, I received a small printed leaflet. After pocketing the paper, I at once departed, being sick and tired of my long entanglement within the "many threaded meshes of an Asylum cobweb," and I do most heartily trust that the "spider of insanity" will never more prey on me again.

Yes, I was now about to exchange homes, the "home of insanity" for the "home of industry," and I was quite willing to do so. There is always a "happy ring" about the word "home"—when it is a happy one!

Of course, it goes without saying that I did not leave the Asylum alone.

It will not come as a surprise to any reader who has followed me thus far, that a little "homely maiden" was waiting to receive me as I emerged from the committee-room. I was not surprised, anyhow. I should have been sadly disappointed if she had not been there.

*　　*　　*　　*　　*　　*

The train we were travelling in had scarcely attained its full speed, when little "homely hands" brought forth a small batch of well-baked cakes. She certainly must have thought that patients leaving asylums required "much sustaining," for the food she brought would have sufficiently satisfied half a dozen school-boys.

While pegging away at the feast provided, the thought struck me that the cakes were, if anything, less homely.

Ah! future events will show that I must have been looking through rose-tinted spectacles that day.

Well, I was just revelling in the knowledge of her improved dough punching, when the train came to a hasty standstill (we had pulled up at a small station). The unexpected vibration caused a slight accident—we not only lost our equilibruim, but our "cakes" also. Down they went, right bang on the floor; and as a traveller opened the carriage door, some went on the platform!

An "obliging porter," almost at the risk of his own life, saved the whole lot from destruction.

Now, if they had chanced to be "sponge cakes," or little bits of "puff paste," we should never have recovered them; but, as it was, they were "homely cakes," therefore we still possessed them.

Before the train again started, I begged my "beloved" to carefully count her "floury handiwork," because if one of those cakes had got under the wheel of a passing carriage, destruction would have been inevitable; they were so "homely."

However, we completed our journey without further accident. Apart from our slight misadventure, everything went on A1 that day—and so did we, too.

FINIS.

LONDON:
PRINTED BY ALEXANDER AND SHEPHEARD,
CHANCERY LANE, W.C.

www.ingramcontent.com/pod-product-compliance
Lightning Source LLC
Chambersburg PA
CBHW020304090426
42735CB00009B/1217